Foundation Curriculum
Copyright © 2014
Written by Linda D. Washington
Illustrated by Rebeca Flott
Edited by Joyce S. Pace and Rita K. Jeffries

STORY BOOK LESSON 2
"THE FALL OF MAN"

Jesus told us to pray and say,
"We pray that Your kingdom will come
that what You want will be done here on earth,
the same as in heaven."

Listen closely to our story to find out why Jesus told us to pray like this!

There is only one God, and He is love. God made everything in the heavens and earth. He also made laws to keep everything in order. God lives in His great kingdom in heaven. A kingdom is where the king who is the leader of everyone lives. No one is higher than God. God is the highest King!

In heaven, God made many angels and gave them minds to think and choose. They were different from Him, but God loved them and called them His sons.

One angel, Lucifer, decided that he wanted to be like God. So he lied and said that he was taking over heaven. Some angels believed him. They chose to obey him and fight the good angels of God. Guess what happened to Lucifer and all the bad angels?

They lost the fight and were kicked out of heaven! The bad angels fell to the earth, away from the love of God. Lucifer did not think about God's love any more. He thought about killing and doing evil things. And he changed into a devil called satan. The bad angels also became devils and demons.

God made the earth ready for you and all His children to live on. He made the first man and named him Adam. God loved Adam. Heavenly Father gave the earth to Adam and his children to be in charge as leaders, and rule it.

God gave man the power to speak words and make everything that was alive on earth obey his words. Even the devil had to obey man's words! Father's plan was for His children on earth to look like Him, and to speak good words that give life and love, just like Him!

Do you remember how Father looks?

Father is a Holy Spirit, and Adam was a spirit also. Adam needed a body to live in, on earth. So your heavenly Father picked up some dust from the ground and shaped it into a body for Adam's spirit to live in. Father breathed into Adam, and the breath of God made Adam a living soul!

Heavenly Father made us in three parts. One, He made us a spirit, like Him! Two, we have a soul. Your soul is your mind that makes choices and your feelings. Three, we have a body for our spirit and soul to live in.

God, Adam's Father, planted a garden in a place called Eden. The garden had many beautiful trees with good food on them. God put Adam inside the garden to take care of it. He told Adam that he could eat from every tree in the garden except one. His Father warned him saying, "You may freely eat from every tree in the garden except the tree of the knowledge of good and evil. You are not to eat from it because on the day that you eat from it, it will become certain that you will die."

God wanted Adam to choose to believe and obey Him. When Father told Adam not to eat from the tree of the knowledge of good and evil, Adam had a choice. He could choose to obey his Father and be the leader of the earth in love. Or, Adam could choose to disobey his Father and die for sure! What would you choose? Listen to the rest of the story to hear what Adam chose.

God saw that Adam was lonely so He put Adam to sleep. God took one of Adam's ribs and made a woman. This woman became Adam's wife and he named her Eve.

One day satan, the devil, came into the garden. He put on the body of a snake to fool Eve.

He said to Eve, "Did God really tell you that you must not eat from any tree in the garden?"
Eve said, "We can eat fruit from the trees of the garden. It's just one tree that we can't eat fruit from!"
The snake said, "You are not going to die!
God knows as soon as you eat it you will learn about good and evil and then you will be
like Him!"

Do you think they should believe the devil?
No! The devil always tells lies!

Adam and Eve were already made to look like and be like God, their Father. They were His children! They already knew good because everything that God made was very good!

Who do you think Adam and Eve believed?

They did NOT believe their Father! They disobeyed Him and ate from the tree of the knowledge of good and evil. The devil had lied and tricked them! Do you remember that God had made laws?

One of God's laws was that whoever you obey becomes your leader and rules over you. Adam and Eve chose to obey and believe the devil! So guess who Adam and Eve had made the leader of the earth? The devil!

Every word that God says is true! God can not lie! He does what He says. So on the day Adam and Eve ate from the tree of knowledge of the good and evil, death came into the world to kill all people that would be born from the seed in Adam. Adam and Eve did not want to think about God's Spirit or God's way of love. They began to think about their bodies and their feelings. Their thinking changed. Their words changed. The things they did changed. And sin and death were on the earth. What do you think their Father is going to say to them?

When Adam and Eve heard God walking in the garden, guess what they did? They hid! God asked them if they ate from the tree that He told them not to eat. Adam said, "The woman who you gave me, she gave me the fruit and I ate it." Have you ever done something and tried to put all the blame on someone else? That's what Adam did.

Adam and Eve had to leave the beautiful Garden of Eden because they did not believe their Father. Do you think He still loved them?

Yes, God is a good Father! He loved Adam and Eve so much that He planned to send His Son Jesus to break and destroy the power of the devil!

After Adam and Eve left the garden, they began to have children. Most of Adam's children would think, say and do bad things which God called sin. Man's spirit was no longer holy like God's Spirit. People no longer wanted to understand the love of God.

Father loves you, but He will not make you choose Him. You have free choice. Father does not want anyone to die or to be hurt by evil. But everyone must choose which kingdom they will obey and belong to, either God's kingdom of love and good

OR the devil's kingdom of sin, darkness, and death.

Which kingdom will you choose?

This is the reason Jesus said to pray for God's kingdom of love and goodness to come back to earth, and for God's will to be done on earth, just like it is in heaven.

The Purpose of the Foundation Curriculum

To firmly establish God's truth in each child's heart early in life so they will understand and know God's love and choose to live fully in the victory that Jesus Christ has already won.

The Goals

To show God's children his love, their true identity as children of God, their authority and power in Christ Jesus, their helper Holy Spirit, and how to pray to their Father in heaven.

THE FALL OF MAN

Story Book Lesson 2

The Objectives to understand from "The Fall of Man" are:

1. Father has a Kingdom in heaven.

2. The bad angels were kicked out of heaven and are on the earth.

3. The leader of the bad angels became the devil.

4. The devil always tells lies.

5. You are a spirit. You have a soul. Your spirit and soul live in your body.

6. Father gave the earth to His children to rule and be the leaders.

7. Father's son Adam (and Eve) believed the lies of the devil.

8. Adam gave the earth to the devil.

9. The devil set up a spirit kingdom on earth.

10. God cannot lie.

11. Father promised to send His Son, Jesus, to save His children on earth.

12. You must choose which kingdom you will serve.

P.A.C.E.
Products and Activities
for Christian Education

For Free Follow-Up Activities to Reinforce This Story Book Lesson Please Visit
www.ABC-Jesus.com

Biblical quotes were from different versions of the holy Bible.

www.ingramcontent.com/pod-product-compliance
Lightning Source LLC
Chambersburg PA
CBHW041551040426
42447CB00002B/144